PEACE FOR THE PROFESSIONAL

A Devotional for the Christian employee working in the secular world.

Author:

Samantha Holmes LPCC-S

ISBN: 9781699499214 (paperback)

No matter if you are a Service Worker or a Celebrity, you have been called by God into your field of work for His Glory. God has made it clear that he is not a respecter of one position over another. God created us all in His image. Caregivers, nurses, supervisors, therapists, writers, politicians, teachers, and 1st responders all have a place in His kingdom. We all make up different and important parts of the body of Christ. God loves the Whole body of His church.

Acknowledgments

◆ ◆ ◆

Thanks be to my God, my Savior Christ Jesus who continues to fill me with peace beyond human understanding. During the hardest storms of my life, God has faithfully comforted me with Philippians 4:7. I couldn't do this work without my Prince of Peace. May the souls who lack you, come to know you too.

Thank you to my loving husband who is the perfect example of a hard-working provider and head of our family. I am ever grateful and often humbled by your dedication, stability, love, and support. You bring trustworthiness into our lives with your work ethics. I love and respect you so much for everything you do for our family. I continue to enjoy seeing all the blessings God is bringing forth in you. Our family is so lucky, simply because you are in our lives. You mean the world to me and our growing family. Selah.

Thank you to my mother who inspires me, because she has been able to make the job of being a mom outshine her career growth. In addition to being a noble and fair leader on the job, you are a woman of noble character and a great mom. Thanks for being a phenomenal woman, mother, grandmother, sister, aunt, and friend. We love you.

Thank you to those family members, friends, pastors, chaplains, mentors, supervisors, co-workers, staff, teachers, and community members who are in my life. You all continue to inspire those around you. You all give hope to the next generation of the workforce. You are all needed and appreciated by so many. Many Blessings to each one of you.

Dedication

This book is dedicated to the working man and woman that has lost hope in their job, their abilities, or themselves.

What happened?

What makes a kind and compassionate worker detest a job they once loved?

What can you do when your own family has needs that your full-time paycheck can't meet?

Who picks up the slack when your exhausted and tomorrows work simply can't wait?

What happens when disaster hits your company and 'all hands on deck' are required to fix it?

What happens when you fail to make your own health visits, because you were helping others from 9-5 m-f?

What happens when you find that you are short on your own fun time funds, because you donated yet again to buy school supplies for your students?

What happens when your true passion doesn't generate revenue? What happens when you need the same financial assistance as your client's, because your salary is below the poverty guidelines too?

What happens when you pour out to others but don't have the energy to pour back into yourself?

HOPEFULLY WHAT HAPPENS IS YOU TAKE THE TIME TO DO SOME SELF-CARE.

Intro:

Because you can never hear it enough.

Professionals, thank you for your service and all you do at work. No matter if you are a teacher, a nurse, a postal worker, or a lawyer. Thank you for every day you show up willing to provide a service to the community you serve. You often make low wages with high risk. You often come in early and leave late. But, thank you for what you do. No matter if you wear uniforms, smocks, or suits, if you are a believer of God at work, you can shine like His living epistle. Thank you for the customer service. Whether you are part-time or full-time, working on the frontline or in the background. Thank you for your willingness to work your shift. Have you been passed over for a promotion after years of hard work? Failed to get the raise but see nepotism prevail? Felt your values and efforts don't match the never-ending demands of your company's? If so, then thank you for continuing to come back to work another day despite the circumstances. I pray you know God has the highest Authority and is the ultimate CEO of the greatest company, The Kingdom of God.

You should know that God is with you, so always put on the full armor of Christ.

Know that you are perfectly created for your position now and the next position God has for you. God is not done molding you into His greatest creation. God's growth in your career cannot be stifled by a job title. People need your gentle loving-kindness and you are an instrument of Christ. Rest assured that your hard work gets you closer to hear 'Well done my good and faithful servant'. No matter what field you are in, if you are a believer, then you are on the front line. This is especially true if you can lead a soul to Christ through excellence in service.Let that sink in. Leading souls to Christ through your excellence in service.

Now that we know the mission, let's talk about the purpose. In this devotional you will hear about some of the battles the American workforce is facing. As you hear the stories of these professionals, look for God's hand in their lives. Listen to how God wants you to persevere in your mind, body, and spirit in your workday, out on the front lines.

I have been working for over 20 years and I've learned how to balance difficult work with meaningful time with my friends and family. I know I am not alone in this difficult juggling act of work, life, and family. Workers all over the world have learned how to stretch their limited resources. Many have learned how to borrow time from the wee hours of the night and some go unpaid to get their jobs done. Many have found that hard work pays off in a variety of unique ways both at home and at work.

◆ ◆ ◆

MONDAY

M ONDAY: *WHO-* 'God do these people even want to get better?'

In the past decade, we have seen a health crisis that affects more than just the health field. Drug use and mental health concerns have been hitting America at record rates. With drug laws and gun laws high on the list of debate around the country, many have asked how to best help their mentally ill or drug addicted loved ones?

In 2017 the Opiate epidemic hit the U.S.A. hard. Drugs like Fentanyl and common prescription medications began taking the lives of thousands each day. Nurses like Mary were finding that people coming in for overdose at the ER were returning days later for the same issue. The medical team had to check to see how recently the last possible overdose had occurred. Mary was no stranger to addiction. She grew up in a home with a mother that abused alcohol. She saw her mother go from PTA president to her biggest embarrassment. Later her mother became her hero when she became sober. Mary's mother had gone to the local Catholic rehab center in the '80s. This was the reason she joined the healthcare field right after high school.

Mary was working a 12-hour shift, she was talking to the sister of the patient she had just revived. He was there for the 2nd time that week. Mary explained to his sister, that he needed to go to rehab. Mary even offered to introduce them to the hospital social worker. She was surprised to hear the response 'We don't need rehab, we need a place with Methadone. We need something to make us feel better.' It was at that moment that Mary realized that the young man and his sister were dealing with the same drug problem.

Mary wondered what could have happened that led two children from the same home to drugs. She remembered seeing her mom suffer from DT's at rehab. She knew that there was power in taking the journey of rehabilitation. Mary's coworker said the siblings were pill shopping. "Have you ever tried rehab before?" Mary asked. She was even more surprised to hear that both the brother and the sister had gone to rehab as teens, already. She learned the two siblings grew up in foster care. They were placed with extended family, and had been in extensive counseling for years. It was then that Mary's supervisor pulled her aside and told her that she had other patients to see. Mary was directed to get them over to social work and move on to her next patient. Mary saw the desperation in the eyes of the young woman who was waiting on her brother to be discharged. Mary was familiar with the chronic, progressive, and fatal disease of addiction. It touched her family years ago. She explained that she would offer to get her into rehab too if she wanted. The girl shouted "That's the problem with doctors. You only want to hospitalize people. You don't want to give them the medications they need to live. We came in to get Methadone. You don't want to help us." The sister got up and pushed her chair in so hard it knocked over Mary's computer.

Mary's coworker and supervisor rushed over. "Are you okay Mary? I can't believe she did that. Coming in here for drugs and blowing up when you offered her help." "I'm going to call security. Don't let them leave before security gets to them." "Addicts are the worse." Mary's coworker and supervisor both meant well, but their tones showed that they were too tired to care anymore. This is a phenomenon called compassion fatigue. If you are serving a challenging population and have found that those you serve are becoming increasingly difficult, this prayer may help you.

God, you have not called me to wrestle against flesh and blood. God help those I encounter to see Your love radiate from inside me. Cover me with your hedge of protection. Keep angels of protection encamped and enthroned around me as go throughout this day. Please step in and intervene. Limit the incidents and keep every soul I encounter safe from harm including my own. Thank you, Lord Jesus, for the blood, you shed on the cross for my safekeeping. Amen.

WHO you serve and who you work next to can affect your spirit as well. Let's take a look at the idea of Unpleasant Co-Workers

While Mary's co-workers meant well, their tones were lacking in love. Love is a key ingredient in working in Godly Excellence on any job. You always want to treat every customer, client, or contact with the love that God has extended to you.

Mary heard her co-workers say negative comments that impacted how she felt inside. How do you handle when the negativity of the day comes from your boss or the office loudmouth sitting next to you?

This prayer is for the worker that has negativity in the workplace. Lord, help me to be the salt and light of my workplace. Help me to be guarded against the murmuring spirit of complaining or judging others. Strengthen my compassion for those I encounter in my workplace. Compassion for my colleagues, leaders, and patrons. Remind me and others that negativity needs none of my attention. Deter the negative voices from my midst. Help me to say kind words of edification that will penetrate and soften the hearts of those that need to hear your still small voice. In Jesus name. Amen.

To learn about the anointing gifts of Mary read John 11:1-37 and Acts 20: 7-12

◆ ◆ ◆

TUESDAY

T UESDAY: *WHAT*- 'What do you want to be when you grow up? What are you going to do after school? What do you see in your five-year plan?' I was asked these questions in 3rd grade, at age 18, and again at age 28 during an interview for career number 2. Never did I think the answer would be, work a job I have lost passion for and struggle financially with life regrets.

Unfortunately, many have these feelings throughout their working years. Some of us have been able to grin and bear it and last decades in a company despite these feelings. For others of us, we weigh the options and keep moving on through our vocational journeys for peace or for pay. Lost passions and financial struggles moved me to over 8 different careers. Ranging from retail, to teacher, to food service, to librarian. At one point the phrase 'You've got the job.' seemed like the inevitable phrase I sought for peace or increased pay after 2 years or so.

This section is for those that had to accept forced vocational journeys. I'd like to share a story about the lost industry. James could honestly say that he liked 2 of his jobs in his entire life. He liked working at the video store and he liked working at the newspaper. Unfortunately for James the video store was phased out in the digital age. (Big win for Neflix and Hulu subscribers, but not for those that worked at the video store Blockbuster.) James bounced back after the video stores closed down. He landed a job at the local paper. After becoming a successful advertisement coordinator, the paper was sold. The merger meant his advertisement position at the newspaper was no longer needed. James tried telemarketing, construction, and eventually retail. He started off at part time seasonal work, and was later offered a full-time position. James ended up buying into his company's 401k and after 5 short years he was fully vested. He worked another 10 years and retired at 55. 15 years at a company that matched and offered profit sharing gave him and his family the retirement he always dreamed of.

Retail work is not always easy. Throughout those 15 years James did a lot of grinning and bearing of it. 'God have you truly called me to do this work?'. James asked himself 5 years into his full-time position. He was expecting his 1st child after 3 years of marriage. He had benefits, a living wage, and the respect of his co-workers. He had accelerated in the position and had received recognition for his excellence in customer service. However, when he would get home he was drained. This was very apparent working at the department store on Black Friday.

James discovered the real meaning of work/life balance on one Black Friday shift. Although he was glad to be off for part of Thanksgiving, he had to go in at 4pm, to prepare the store for the midnight door buster crowd (that actually came at 8pm).

James wanted to tell the demanding customers 'Don't you know the true meaning of the holiday season?'. On this day he often helped in departments that he didn't work in. The store thought having more workers there would help to ease the panic of shoppers looking for midnight deals and bargains. This was after all the most affordable shopping day of the year. James was not a fan of the commercialism of holidays. But, he never reminded the customers that they had lived without these items all year long. In his mind, they could probably continue to live without it. Inside James was thinking about his own soon to be new arrival. James was thinking about how he would feel if he couldn't afford the crib or the stroller/car seat set that he and his wife purchased months ago. He even smiled when he saw a couple looking for a play pen and shared that his wife had bought one online earlier, but didn't get the 20% discount they would get for the midnight deal. He assured them that they were getting a great bargain and that they would find the assembly was a breeze. One brief encounter with a customer revealed the blessings some find when buying things they needed all year, but couldn't afford on a low salary. His thinking shifted. James recalled what he was thankful for. He was thankful to have stability after watching the industrial changes of his generation. Even though he was not a rock star like he said at age 18 and was not a cop like he said he would be at age 8. He was told by that couple that he was a good sales clerk. He also had heard from his wife that he was a great husband and he would be an even better father. James was glad for the kiss he got from his wife that next morning thanking him for working hard to make their life easier. Her brother and uncle actually put together the crib that James read was easy to assemble in a breeze. That kiss and the love of his family meant more to him than all the fun he had at the video store and at the newspaper. He was even thankful that he had a chance to take his then girlfriend (now wife) for a late night view of the video store years ago. When he surprised her that night with a preview of a movie she was waiting to see, he knew she would be his wife. If you are struggling with a job that feels mundane try this prayer.

Father God help me to bloom where I am planted. I thank you Lord for my work/life journey. Help me find the ability to appreciate what I am doing for my community and for my family through this work I do. Help reveal to me how my everyday work supports those I encounter. Give me wisdom on how to progress and navigate on my job, so I can achieve stability. Lord allow my work to bring forth a yield of prosperity for my family's needs. Strengthen my work ethic Lord so I can do even the hardest parts of this job in excellence. God continue to show me my purpose here and make it clear when or if I am meant to move both laterally and vertically. In Jesus name I pray. Amen.

Remember WHAT you do while at work is also a reflection of your belief system.

God's laws are clear. Challenge yourself to look at the way you conduct business. If you find any sign of impropriety, repent and be mindful of how you represent God in the workplace. James in our story luckily did not give into temptation and ruin his customers holiday cheer. Rather than complain he abstained from selfish murmuring and focused on the goodness of God.

James 5:9 Do not complain, brethren, against one another, so that you yourselves may not be judged; behold, the Judge is standing right at the door. (NIV)

To learn more about blooming where you are planted. Study the book of James in the bible. James chapters 2-5 talks about equal treatment and the reward for hard work. James identified himself as having a servanthood work ethic, seeking to glorify God not himself.

◆ ◆ ◆

WEDNESDAY

WEDNESDAY: *WHEN* – 'God, I just can't go in there tonight'.

Let's start with the basic fact. There is only 24 hours in a day. Most of us hope to work 8, sleep 8, and spend the remaining 8 doing things we want and need to do.

But, what happens when you work overtime and miss time with your family? The 2nd and 3rd shift can be grueling hours. Swing shift and Grave yard shift are common names for the late night working hours. These workers leave their home at 7pm and finish their shift at 5am. They go in to work at 4am and leave work at 2pm, too tired to help kids with homework. These work hours can be taxing on the wake/sleep pattern and the work/life balance.

Martha was a dispatcher who worked 2nd and 3rd shift

most nights. She'd been doing this work for nearly 10 years when her sister died in 2016. The night shift always felt familiar to her, because she always enjoyed the night life when she was younger. Martha and her sister were 3 years apart. She remembered that when she and her sister were young they dreamed of working the late night shift. They wanted to be like their parents. However they wanted to come home to spend those days with their families, instead of sleeping. Martha never married and never had kids. Her time with family was often a quick visit with her sister, mom and nieces, during the day. She rarely missed a school recital or a field trip with the girls. She thought of herself as the fun aunt. Her family still lived in the community where she had grown up.

Martha made it a point to visit all the neighborhood landmarks with her nieces when she could. She took them to the swings at the park, the neighborhood store for candy, and the local restaurant for turnovers before dinner. Over the years Martha heard that crime and violence was impacting her community.

Martha worked as a dispatcher. So often she heard calls and saw officers go out to respond to crime happening late at night. Sometimes she heard about the calls that happened during the day, when the other dispatchers text her about what was happening in her area. Martha had a close relationship with one particular officer, Gary who worked in her community. The two were very fond of one another. Gary grew up in the neighborhood too. He lived on the other side of the park. From time to time, Martha invited Gary to spend time with her and her family at school events for the nieces. He even came out to get those 'before dinner' turnovers.

Martha was out with Gary and other city workers celebrating a retirement when she got the call about her sister's death. Martha's sister was murdered in 2016. Martha started blaming herself for not moving her family out of the old neighborhood. Martha wished she had been wiser with her money. She watched her parents work so hard and earn so little. Her parents worked at a local hotel when she was young. They cleaned the lobby, pool, and banquet halls late at night after the guests were in bed. This is why they were so tired during the day. Her mom and nieces had joined her that night at the retirement party. She remembers hearing her colleagues and her mother talking about the 2016 election. That was when she got the text. The city was being rumored to start mandatory overtime, as a result of the election outcome. She was considering volunteering to do the overtime, for the extra money. Others were outraged about longer shifts. When she got the text, from her dispatcher friend. It said Is anyone at your home now? She was told that something happened in her neighborhood. Gary also got the text, they decided to go over to her house together. When they arrived, they saw that her sister had been shot and was bleeding.

She still can't remember all the details from that day, and even now it is painted red with anger, blood, and regrets. Sometimes Martha would get sick to the stomach when she would get a call from her neighborhood. One of neighbors was arrested for a break in. She took the call for an ATM hit and grab that happened at the restaurant where they got the turnovers. She knew the person and always suspected him of being involved with her sister's murder. Although, it was never proven. This same neighbor was said to have been associated with another murder in their town. But he was never charged for that crime either. Martha's sister's murder is still unsolved to this day.

Martha began drinking more that year after the murder. She started having nightmares and found it hard to sleep. She started working overtime and was seeing her nieces less and less. Martha and officer Gary often went out for drinks and talked about the crime in the community. That was how she spent most of that first year after her sister died. Instead of visiting her nieces after school or before dinner they would meet at the city worker pub or hang out. One day, Gary said to Martha: "You haven't been to see your girls in a while,

I hear." "Aren't you off today? I heard the school has a play going on. You used enjoy spending time with the girls. I know they would love to see you.". Martha replied that she was off, but she was going to work the double shift. She was still saving to buy that house for her mother and nieces to move. She found the double shifts and drinks helped her sleep just long enough to get a quick snooze. And the extra pay seemed to help with saving for the down payment on the house.

Gary grew worried after a few failed attempts to get Martha back connected with her nieces. Gary eventually told Martha and her mother about EAP counseling. He told her how it was offered through the city, and gave her, her mother, and her nieces access to 7 free sessions with a counselors. The service also provided free access to financial consultants. Gary explained how they could help her with the home buying experience. Gary had used the service when he bought his house. Martha was interested in the home buying, but was unsure if she needed to talk to the counselors about her loss. Since she wanted the girls to be able to talk to someone, she finally gave them a call. She was linked to a grief counselor and alcohol treatment center the same day she made the call. Martha took some time off work and began counseling for PTSD, Bereavement, and Alcohol Use Disorder. Martha is now working regular hours again and discovered she qualified for a down payment incentive. After a few months she bought that home for her family.

We all have family matters outside of work. We all will lose loved ones and will have our personal ways of dealing with it. No matter if personal grief has overcome you or if you are working more and spending less time with family, this prayer may help.

Heavenly father you know my pain and you know my afflictions. You promised to be the help in time of need. You are the great comforter. I need your comfort now. Lord please take away the pain I am carrying each day at work and at home. Replace my emptiness and ashes with beauty and joy. Help me to remember all the reasons to give you praise. You have given me more than enough. I thank you for the good times I have had with my loved ones, and ask for opportunities to connect with those still in my life. I believe you will restore my spirit again to enjoy those loving friends and family more fully Lord. Lord please bring forth new joy like the newness in the sun rising each day. Thank you for waking me up this morning and giving me every one of these hours in your blessed day. I need more of You Lord, to keep me going this day and the next. I ask that you fill my cup with the overflowing oil of restoration as I consider what has been taken away, what has been given, and what wonderful things have been left behind for me to enjoy today. Thanks be to my Glorious King Emanuel. You are with me every day of my life especially on the hardest days. Help me make the most of my time on earth Lord and connect in a more meaningful way to those in front of me when I can. In Jesus name I pray. Amen

Jesus explains it this way.

Matthew 26:11 'The poor [the sick and the needy] you will always have with you, but you will not always have me.'

Remember to keep the Sabbath holy and spend time with those you love *WHEN* you can. Also consider counseling if your personal life is so heavy you avoid it with work or other distractions. Look in the glossary at the end of this book for tips on how to find a licensed therapist/counselor in your area.

◆ ◆ ◆

THURSDAY

THURSDAY: *WHERE – 'God this is a difficult environment. How can I ever go back in here?'*

Jimmy had been a plumber for 19 years by the time he was 35. When he finished high school, he was already an apprentice in the plumbing field. His uncle encouraged him to go to the technical high school to learn the trade. The family had a business and most of them were members of the local plumbers union. He was grateful at age 18 to be making a decent salary. He didn't go to college, so he had no student loan debt. He had a nice sports car. But, he didn't go out much and was a bit of a loner. Jimmy was always uncomfortable in social settings. He had a speech impediment and would stutter at times. But, when he was plumbing he worked alone. He was anxious about his stutter and would sometimes get facial tics. They got worse when he thought others noticed it.

Jimmy felt good about his ability to do well in his job. He was also glad he didn't have to spend more years in school sitting in front of a college classroom. Jimmy felt like he was a man in his family home. He took on responsibilities and helped out his father and uncle with home projects regularly. Jimmy was well liked by the other plumbers and his family was proud of him when he became a journey level plumber after only 2 years on the job. Although Jimmy was respected for his work, he was teased often about needing to settle down and find a wife. However, Jimmy believed it would happen when he was really ready.

Jimmy came into a job one Friday, and was greeted by a husband who explained that he was heading off to work and his wife would be there while the plumbing job was going on. When Jimmy met the wife briefly he fantasized for a moment about having his own wife and family. He hoped his wife would be attractive. He did his best not to look at her walking around the house cleaning and preparing food. Working inside the homes of other people made him nervous. Being stared at by customers was always his greatest fear and least favorite part of his work.

Jimmy was moving along on the job and then splash; a stream of water was pouring out onto the floor. He had forgot to re-tighten the water supply line. The entire bathroom and kitchen flooded in seconds.

Jimmy was scared. He thought about his family business being sued and the family losing their 40-year company in a law suit. The wife seemed to appear out of nowhere. Saying: "There's some water in the kitchen". Jimmy apologized and tried to move as fast as he could saying: "It was all my fault". The wife just grabbed a mop and a few rags and helped get the water cleaned up. There was something about her that was peaceful. Jimmy was still nervous that the husband would come back to see the water damage and call the company to file a complaint. Or worse a law suit. Jimmy and the wife finally got the water cleaned up. He knew he was to blame and he still had to come back to finish the rest of the job. Most of the day was dedicated to cleaning up the water. Jimmy was a mess that entire week and dreaded going back to the home where he knew he had caused something like $5000 in damages. Jimmy was expecting to be handed an estimate of the damages by the husband. When he arrived for the 2nd half of the job, Jimmy was careful to not drag his tools and machinery on the nice hardwood floors. The floors looked nice and the damages were not as bad as he remembered. He felt faint when he heard the husband coming down to the basement stairs where he was working. His anxiety and stuttering got worse and he could barely get out the words: "I'm sorry about last week". The husband said "Hey man, You know I bought this house 5 years ago. Me and wife could hardly afford those 1st few years and eventually she told me she was ready to have kids. I was terrified thinking how can we have kids when we can't even afford the upkeep of this house." Jimmy got a huge lump in his throat. Then he heard the husband explain: "My wife has tremendous faith. She always told me that Grace and Mercy were her favorite traits of God." "Well, my wife is actually pregnant right now, and we like the names Grace and Mercy for a girl. Michael for a boy. That's a nice strong name isn't it." Jimmy tried to smile. He could feel his face trembling. Then he felt the greatest weight lifted when the husband explained how everyone makes mistakes from time to time. He went on to say how we all just need a break every now and then. He asked Jimmy how long the job would take, because he was going to paint over the walls. And wanted to do another summer project. Jimmy learned that the husband did call his family's company and they sent out a cleaning crew to refinish the floors. The family also had a home warranty that would cover the cost of some of the damages. The difference was credited to the family along with gift cards to a furniture store. Jimmy did his best work that day.

Who would have thought that after he had the worst day of his plumbing career, he'd get redemption and a second chance? If you have made a mistake at work and have fears about the consequences, Try this prayer.

Heavenly Father, I repent for falling short of your Glory. I know that I am not perfect and I have made an error at work. If you see fit for me to have Grace and Mercy in this job, please extend it fully for me. I thank you that your blood and your love can cover a multitude of sins. I ask that you show me how to be humble, admit my faults, and to make amends as I look to you for an opportunity to grow from this mistake. Help me to be better at seeking you before I speak, think, act, do and create in the workplace. God I know that any discipline I get at work will never compare to the attack you endured when you shed blood for my sins. I ask that You help me to understand how to best use Your grace and mercy to improve my work ethics next time. In Jesus name I pray. Amen.

Consider the book of James if you need more guidance on grace and mercy in the workplace.

James 4:6-10 6 But he gives us more grace. That is why Scripture says: "God opposes the proud but shows favor to the humble."[7] Submit yourselves, then, to God. ...[8] Come near to God and he will come near to you. Wash your hands, you sinners, and purify your hearts, you double-minded.[9] Grieve, mourn and wail. Change your laughter to mourning and your joy to gloom.[10] Humble yourselves before the Lord, and he will lift you up.

God knows better than anyone, all the many ways we humans can mess up. We all fall short of the glory of God. None of us are perfect even if we are great in our work, we are still only human. We all have limits and faults. Because we will all fall short of God's glory, we must be prepared to be told about our faults when we mess up in the workplace. When you have that dreaded meeting with your boss. Or you hear complaints made about you at work. Just know, you can get through anything if you are prepared to be humble and accept grace and mercy from the Almighty God Jehovah.

◆ ◆ ◆

FRIDAY

FRIDAY: *WHY –'God Why?'*

Sometimes there are many aspects of the job that can overwhelm you. Jerry has been a salesman, since the '90s he learned about the benefits of an honest handshake and a genuine smile. He'd read all the books on sales and was passionate about closing the deal. He appreciated the referrals and the life long customers that came with the business. Then his industry was hit with the auto bailout of 2008. He was told by the dealership that his lot was closing and all inventory would be sent over to the other side of town. Senior salesmen like Jerry were offered the option of taking a severance package. But they would lose a % of retirement vesting. The other option was they could apply at the other sales lot for a similar position. Jerry's good friend took the payout, and went into early retirement. Jerry decided to apply at the other office because he was still trying to pay for college tuition for his son. Jerry was glad when they offered him a sales position at the other car lot. He'd gone over to the other office for staff meetings and felt he knew the team well enough. His wife was glad to hear that he was offered a job too. For Jerry, this would mean a 45 minute commute to get to work in the morning. He'd also have a 45 minute commute back home. But hey, at least he had a job and could get to 65, pay for the last year of college, and retire.

The first few months were fine. Jerry enjoyed the long commutes and the peace of his drive. Then winter hit. Jerry's 45 minute commute became over an hour each way. Not to mention the dangerous driving conditions. Jerry lived near the snow belt and was hit hard with weather most of the winter. The other side of town was always much clearer when he arrived, but he dreaded his ride back home. Jerry was grateful for a job, it paid the bills and kept him and his family covered with provisions. One wintery weekend morning Jerry's car hit a patch of ice and landed in a snow bank. Jerry was glad to be alive, but he was no more than a few miles from home and nowhere near his job. He called in to let his boss know he was going to need the day off, because he was in a snow bank and waiting on a tow. 'Wow there's no snow out here.' His boss replied. 'How close are you? We can send someone out to get you if you need a lift in'. Jerry decided that he would rather go back home, because the weather conditions were expected to get worse. Jerry had spectacular attendance at the old car lot. He was usually on time or early most days. Some mornings he even had time to grab donuts for the staff and customers on his way in. The new location required several adjustments to his routine to get there each day. Jerry sat in his car and remembered the old car lot days. The tow truck came and Jerry went home in a rental car. He was greeted by his wife who was grateful, but shocked to see him home so early. Jerry spent the afternoon with her looking for jobs closer to home, but didn't find much in the line of car sales.

After the accident, Jerry went from having perfect attendance, to being 25 minutes to an hour late most days. Jerry was finding that he was so stressed that he even lost his charm with his customers. He struggled with hitting his sales numbers and was placed on probation for attendance and performance. He seemed disconnected from the customers on this new side of town. When he'd see an old customer or a familiar face come over and ask him how he liked working in the new location, Jerry would smile and say 'It's going well'. Even though he was on probation for work performance and attendance. Jerry's health was declining and he was finding he was not sleeping and was feeling tired most of the time. He was even caught sleeping at his desk once.

Within a few months of the accident, Jerry was called into the Executive office of the dealership. The upper management told him that he was going to be let go. Jerry's blood rushed to his head and he was flooded with fear, anger, and shock. Jerry had worked in the industry since the late '70s. He saw decades of change happen at the dealership, and watched the auto industry get bailed out. Jerry could not believe he was being let go after all these years. He felt angry that the company had no loyalty to the staff. He felt like he had earned them more money than they ever paid him throughout his career. He was hurt that he was terminated while on probation and not given enough time to fix the issue. Jerry resented the space he was given when he came over to the new office. He was no longer given the front desk, allowing for regular customer traffic at the dealership. Jerry felt like the moment he was sent over to this new car lot, he was set up for failure. He wondered about his wife and family and how he was going to pay for the college tuition for his son. Jerry was mad. He was mad at his company and mad at himself. "Why didn't I take the severance package like the others?" Jerry thought to himself. He wished he had quit before they could fire him. Jerry cleared his desk and barely said a word to the co-workers that were offering him a hand with carrying his boxes to the car. He drove a long ride home and when he pulled into the driveway at midday he shouted out "God Why?". He wondered if his wife would ask him about why he was home so early.

Jerry went on unemployment for a little over a year. He spent many days thinking about the job, because he'd worked at that dealership during the most monumental times of his life. He had two, foot surgeries there and raised his son while working at the company. He felt defeated leaving the work force at 63. He wanted to wait those last two years to maximize his retirement payout. He told his wife he might get a part time job just to have more money. He considered driving for Uber to get more money to go along with the adjusted severance and unemployment. One week of driving for Uber quickly sent Jerry away from ride sharing. Jerry had no idea what to do for work even after a year of being unemployed. He showed proof of applying to jobs to get the unemployment benefits. But even the few places that did call him for an interview seemed skeptic of hiring him. Jerry felt like he was no longer a part of the work force. Some days he felt so humbled seeing kids go to school, and neighbors return home from work. He eventually found it in his heart to clear the snow off the neighbors car before they went to work. He would clear the sidewalks near the park so the kids had a safe passage to the bus stop.

After a Year on unemployment Jerry realized that he would still have been commuting 45 minutes and would be miserable if he had not been let go. Jerry imagined all the health risks and car accidents he avoided because he was home and not on the road.

Jerry enjoyed that he did not have to request time off to spend time celebrating his son's college graduation. Jerry learned to be grateful for what was given, taken away, and left behind. Between his unemployment benefits, the severance package, and his savings, Jerry managed to budget just enough to keep his life on track. Him and his family survived, the bills were met, and they all learned to accept some minor lifestyle changes.

Shortly after that year of unemployment, Jerry got a call from his old friend who had accepted the payout. Jerry learned that the payout money went by fast and his friend was relying on only the social security benefits. He too had to find a 2nd form of income. His friend had started a snow removal and landscape company. Jerry was asked if he wanted to do a project with maintaining the grounds at a nearby church. Apparently, there was a grant for the upkeep of historic churches. Jerry took the project for the year and then decided to continue. He continued to volunteer with his friend and got some additional side jobs as a result of the congregation admiring the work he was doing. Jerry shares his testimony about the Godly intervention of the auto crisis.

If you have been terminated or you are worried about being fired, try this Prayer.

Father God. This change was unwanted, unexpected, and has been devastating. I know that you now all things including how I will come out victorious with this battle. Lord you know how I have felt defeated at times since losing this position, please help me find the strength to get through. God please take over this battle for me and my family because I know You always win. God while, I fear of the unknown, about where resources will come in, please remind me that you are Jehovah Jireh. I ask that you provide for every need my family and I have and help us to lack no good thing. God You always makes a way. God help me not to be bitter or jealous of others. Help me to realize how to let go of making my identity about work and rather focus on being the kind of person that is good to others. Lord help me to let go of what I thought I once needed and find comfort and satisfaction in my free time with you. God help me to let go of my anger about not having a say about my last job. Soften my heart and help me learn what is needed for my next phase. Help me be more attune to your voice and understand the next opportunities you have for me. God, I ask that you will help me see how You have done for me what I could not and would not do for myself. I thank You Lord and give you praise despite my circumstances.

God help me to find peace during my transition. In Jesus name. Amen.

For more guidance and dealing with unexpected work changes read Jeremiah and Romans.

Jeremiah 29:11 New International Version (NIV) 11 For I know the plans I have for you, declares the Lord, plans for welfare and not for evil. To give you a future and a hope.

Romans 8:28 New International Version 28 And we know that in all things God works for the good of those who love him, who have been called according to his purpose.

For helpful tips on benefits and entitlements that can get you through the season of unemployment consider calling your local United Way office, or visit www.211.org for more information.

◆ ◆ ◆

SATURDAY

S ATURDAY: *HOW "God how did this person even get a job here?*

When controversial topics happen outside work, it can seep into the office doors. We know that Iron sharpens Iron, and we are responsible for what we say in and out of work. It is important to remember that we are walking epistles for many in the work place.

A harsh boss is just one way to describe someone that micromanages, criticizes, and is unappreciative of your efforts in the work place. Let's make it clear that hurt people hurt people. Some of us are just better than others at managing our pain. If you are like many of us, you have learned how to put on a good face and plug away at the job. But what happens when you can't deal with your overdemanding job any longer?

Pete was a painter that did off site jobs for a local paint retail company. He had learned the skills of painting from his grandfather in his youth. He started out in sales at the paint company. He began helping customers select their paint colors. Later he became a paint mixer, customizing the colors for businesses and residents alike. Over the past 12 years, he'd gotten familiar with most aspects of the work. He was trained in applying paint, completing dry wall repairs, and even in finding contractors for big projects. Pete was a natural at this work. He recalled the lessons he got from his grandfather about doing home repairs. He took pride in every aspect of the work. He knew how to make his paint strokes clean and how to prevent errors when doing home repair jobs.

When he was 1st hired for this position he was told some weekend hours were required. This was described in the interview, as 1 Saturday a month. Pete was coming home tired for the 5th Saturday in a row. He was really starting to resent his boss Mr. Ned who seemed to assume he had no weekend plans or a life for that matter. Pete once overheard Mr. Ned say he didn't ask the employees with families to do regular weekend overtime. Although Pete was single, he enjoyed spending time with his girlfriend and her 11 year old daughter because he considered them his family. Both of them enjoyed having dinner with their parents on the weekend.

Pete did consider himself to be a family man, even though he was not married. Pete and his girlfriend both lived in the same community. Pete was considered a handyman around the neighborhood. He took pride in doing projects for his neighbors and the people who lived in his community. Pete was planning to propose to his girlfriend this year. He was using the overtime money he got from weekends to save up to buy a ring. But 5 weekends in a row was not easy. Pete had other projects, family matters, and a 10-year relationship to attend to.

Some weekends were not so bad, if Pete was there alone or working with another colleague. However, when Mr. Ned was there he was always very negative. He always found a way to double the workload. One weekend, he asked Pete to drive back to the store to get basic color samples to show a family. The problem was that they had already selected a customized color. In fact, Pete remembered that he customized their color 2 years ago. When he made the color for them, they were delighted to hear he could mix that same color for them again if they wanted. Why couldn't Mr. Ned just listen? "This looks like dry wall. Tear it down." Ned shouted at Pete. As it turns out it was not dry wall, and the business was upset when Ned had to call in another contractor to repair the damages. Pete couldn't begin to count how many times Mr. Ned would ask him to go and correct error projects. 'He's the boss shouldn't he know what he is doing? How does he make such poor executive decisions? Why do I have to clean up all his messes?' Pete would ask himself. Pete wondered if some of Ned's motivation was just to drive up the hours and charges to the customers. "This is highway robbery. Another two days?" some customers would say. Pete knew Ned charged the customers by the hour. Pete would hear Mr. Ned berate both him and sometimes even the customers. Pete hated the weekends with Mr. Ned and he was one of the few employees that would even agree to do the overtime during weekend hours.

Pete found Mr. Ned to be offensive and harsh. Pete was even considering leaving the job and starting his own handyman service. One Saturday, Pete was able to see Mr. Ned actually get his hands dirty instead of make demands. The job was a big one. A local business was re-branding and needed the entire front lobby repainted to match their new logo. Pete wanted to finish, to go home and meet Janet, his girlfriend. This was their unofficial anniversary. The two had started dating a few years after high school, when his grandfather died. Janet was always close to his family. Pete and his grandfather had done countless home projects for Janet's family over the years. Her parents supported him and his family when Pete's grandfather died. Both Pete and Janet valued family. That's what he loved most about her.

As Mr. Ned tipped over a can of paint onto the plastic. Pete rushed over and grabbed the paint scrape and the roller and got most of the excess up from the drop cloth. "Thanks", Ned said to Pete with a harrumph. This was the 1st time he can recall Mr. Ned ever saying thanks or ever saying anything even remotely kind for that matter. Mr. Ned shared that he had lost his wife to cancer a few years ago. Ned said the old logo of this company reminded him of the 1st date he had with his wife. Pete listened. Mr. Ned shared about the time he spent with his wife and the pain of watching her lose her health battle to cancer 2 years ago.

Pete remembered, because he went to the funeral with the other staff. Obviously, Ned never noticed he was there. Then Mr. Ned said something that shocked Pete. You had a nice girl with you at the funeral. Word around the store is that you are planning to marry her. Yes, Pete was a little apprehensive to admit this to Ned. The phrase 'Ned never noticed.' was a common one amongst the employees. It seemed no matter how good of a job you did or how much you were going through, that Mr. Ned never noticed. Even if he did, he was probably going to complain and demand even more.

Pete and Mr. Ned finished the work that Saturday. Pete learned that Ned thought he was one of the best paint-ers and that is why he asked him out so often on the

Weekends. Ned shared that he has seen that Pete was gifted years ago, and was glad when he applied for this department 2 years ago. Ned and Pete talked about the pains of life, including Ned's trials and errors in the industry. Ned admitted that he was starting to get arthritis in his hands and couldn't do the work as well as he used to. Ned didn't become any less of a tyrant around the company, but Pete did find the humanity inside the hard exterior of the man.

Later that month, Pete did propose to his girlfriend. He went down to part time at the paint shop and started his own local handyman service. Pete found that with the two part time jobs, he actually had more time to spend with his family including some weekends. Pete and his wife Janet are now happily married and moved in on the same block as their parents. Not all difficult bosses will make the effort to try like Mr. Ned. Some folks seem to delight in misery. If you have a negative or offensive leader, you have a right to report anyone including a boss to HR. And, for the covert spiritual attacks, you can always pray.

Try this prayer if you work for someone that is harsh and critical towards you or others:

> God I thank you for the shield of faith. May every aspect of my day be covered. You already have won the victory over evil. I am grateful to

be on the winning side. Lord send your angels to surround and protect those I come in contact with. Cover us with your hedge of protection. Prepare the workplace to be receptive of the kind words you have deposited in me. Lord help me water the seeds of goodness that have already been deposited in your good people. Lord you know the needs of your people including those who have negativity. God I know you never give us more than we can bear. I accept your assignment to spread Kingdom love in my workplace. May others be drawn towards you by my attitude. I thank you for the helmet of Salvation and the Gospel of peace. Help me to use the Living Word to respond to verbal attacks and false accusations made towards me or others. I know that the battle is already won. Lord please allow the breastplate of righteousness to safekeep those that Love You. Help me to know when to depart in silence and when to respond with a public correction. Help me to see where I should end and You should begin. I ask for discernment and wisdom to help me navigate in this environment. God please make it clear, when my assignment has ended and if you wish for me to step away from this workplace. Guide me in your righteous ways throughout my vocational journey. In Jesus Name I pray. Amen.

Try studying about Peter in Acts. Also review Ephesians and the Proverbs to help you discern what direction to take with a harsh boss.

> *Proverbs 15:1 New International Version (NIV) 1 A gentle answer turns away wrath, but a harsh word stirs up anger.*

> *Proverbs 27:17 New International Version (NIV) 17 As iron sharpens iron, so one person sharpens another.*

> *Ephesians 6:14-17 New International Version (NIV)[14] Stand firm then, with the belt of truth buckled around your waist, with the breastplate of righteousness in place,[15] and with your feet fitted with the readiness that comes from the gospel of peace.[16] In addition to all this, take up the shield of faith, with which you can extinguish all the flaming arrows of the evil one.[17] Take the helmet of salvation and the sword of the Spirit, which is the word of God.*

God will never call you to go into a literal battle at work. But you will need to learn strategies for navigating the work field if you want to keep your peace. Request a copy of the HR bullying policies if you feel you have been mistreated or targeted in your work place.

◆ ◆ ◆

SUNDAY

S UNDAY: *HOW MUCH?* - "I can barely live off this Salary. God there has to be something else out there for me."

If you are like many Americans, you are over worked and under paid. The underpaid part can sometimes feel like an understatement, when you look at the cost of living increases. In 2012 a campaign was started in New York City to fight for a minimum wage increase to $15 nationally. This campaign is for fast food service workers, home health aides, child care providers, retail workers, and college professors. Skilled laborers and non-skilled laborers alike experience underemploy-ment. Underemployed describes those individuals that have gainful employment, but are close to, or below federal poverty guidelines. The term 'living wage' often does not allow for many to achieve the basic ne-cessities of life, such as child care, nutritional food, or health care. Political analysts have recently started looking at how privatized companies are making more corporate decisions that try to support the gaps that government programming miss. In a democracy, we should remember that voting and the power of the collective voice can help make lasting social change in work force benefits. I will caution that you should take extreme care when it comes to participating in unorganized strikes at your workplace. The simplest collective voice opportunity may be your local voting polls. But, for more information on the success of the Fight for $15 movement go to www.fightfor15.org

After she retired from working in the school cafeteria, Paula was now a proud grandmother. She was also a widow. Within a few months of her retirement, she gained custody of her two grandchildren. This was around the time her son went to jail. Paula thought her working years were behind her. Then she learned that the money from fostering her grandchildren was not enough to maintain the household of 3. Paula was a simple woman. After her husband died, she moved into a smaller home. She went from a 3-bedroom house to a single-bedroom apartment with a pullout coach for guests. She never knew that her two grandchildren may have to make that pullout coach their home for a season. Although the kids were small they were growing fast. The two could no longer sleep in the pullout comfortable. She wanted to get a rollaway bed to make the home more functional. When looking in her favorite department for the fold away, she noticed the hiring sign in the window. Paula decided to go back to work at age 69.

When she sat in the interview at the local department store, she was told that if she was hired she would get a discount on the clothes. This was a blessing Paula thought to herself. Paula had shopped here to get her grandkids countless Christmas and birthday gifts. She liked the products and appreciated the idea of getting a discount. Paula saw the kids tease and taunt each other when she worked in the cafeteria. She didn't want her grandchildren going without clothes and getting their needs met. She often shopped at this department store. This store offered discounted name brand clothes and shoes as well as countless household items. She felt good seeing her two grandchildren well dressed and well cared for. Paula got the job offer, and when she started she was trained by a woman named Cathy. The only part of the training with Cathy that rattled her, was when she was asked how she would handle customers stealing from her store. Cathy was loud, and sometimes off putting. Most customers and staff avoided her, unless she was opening up a new line for checking out.

Cathy called Paula outside one day and explained to her that the store was getting ready to throw away unsold merchandise. Paula recalled that the policy was that if merchandise was getting thrown out, due to lack of sales that the employees could purchase it at ½ the lowest price. Cathy on the other hand, just wanted to load the merchandise into her car. Cathy said it was going to be thrown in the dumpster anyway. Cathy went on about how "even at ½ price, some of the merchandise is still too expensive". Even though some of the merchandise was overpriced in Paula's opinion, it was clear that the stores policy forbid them from taking merchandise off the premises without purchasing. Even if they were in the dumpsters. Paula walked away and went back inside to finish her lunch break. On her way back in, Paula saw 2 rollway beds in the unsold merchandise area. But, it was still too expensive for Paula to purchase that day. Paula knew she had no intentions of stealing like Cathy was doing. She asked her manager about the employee layaway policy, and Paula was pleased to hear she could get the rollaway beds added to layaway with no money down. She took them home in less than 2 paychecks. A few months later she saw Cathy being escorted out of the store in handcuffs. She had been seen on camera taking merchandise out of the store dumpsters and loading it into her car.

It goes without saying that, "Thou shall not steal." Ex 20:15 (NIV)

However, we all have needs and need a living wage.

Please know that God has not called you to do anything that is against his kingdom principals or the natural law of the land.

Habakkuk 2:6-7 New International Version (NIV) 'Woe to him who piles up stolen goods
and makes himself wealthy by extortion!
How long must this go on?'⁷ Will not your creditors suddenly arise?
⁷Will they not wake up and make you tremble?
Then you will become their prey.'

Paula was wise to look for legal ways to get her needs met.

Psalm 34:10 New International Version (NIV) "those who trust in the Lord lack no good thing."

Paula was not seeking out to serve her own selfish needs but was hoping to make provisions for her family. She was extending her small home to those who were in need. We know that God loves a cheerful giver and to whom much is given much is required.

When you are faced with financial hardship remember the generosity of the Woman who gave the small copper coins.

Luke 21:1-4 New International Version (NIV) "As Jesus looked up, he saw the rich putting their gifts into the temple treasury.[2] He also saw a poor widow put in two very small copper coins.[3] "Truly I tell you," he said, "this poor widow has put in more than all the others.[4] All these people gave their gifts out of their wealth; but she out of her poverty put in all she had to live on."

Consider how you can bless others, rather than seeking to gain more income. Trust God's abundance and practice generosity towards those in your life. Organizations like the fight for $15 use the bible's economic system where the 1st shall be last and the last shall be 1st. When writing to the church of Phillipi, Paul said:

Phil 4:11-13 New International Version (NIV) for I have learned to be content whatever the circumstances.[12] I know what it is to be in need, and I know what it is to have plenty. I have learned the secret of being content in any and every situation, whether well fed or hungry, whether living in plenty or in want.[13] I can do all this through him who gives me strength.

Look for the ways you are abundant in your life. Use what God has given you to advance your family and the kingdom of God, and count every blessing you have. God has more in store for your finances when you budget for Him and not out of your lack.

Whatever job you are on, remember to do your work with integrity and follow your company's policy, standards, and guidelines. If you are finding that your wage does not meet your day to day needs, then consider this prayer:

Lord in the name of your son Jesus, I humbly ask for your protection and provision. God, I am believing for an increase, unexpected blessings, and favor during this tough financial time. I am thankful for all you have made available for me and my family's needs. You are Jehovah Jireh and I know you can provide where I see lack. Help me to be a good steward over what you have given me. Give me wisdom and strength for my family's survival in this financial storm. I am grateful that You make provisions for your people. I pray that no good thing be withheld from my family because you know each of our individual needs. God, You have never forsaken me, and I know that you love me. Help me to remember that every penny you provide has a purpose. God show me how to work smarter with my time, money, and talents so that I can see increase and abundance. Help me to find ways to continue to do good for the Kingdom, despite my finances. Help me to see clearly what direction you have for me as you are preparing me and my family for our increase season. Lord help me to stay connected to you and know that you reward those that diligently seek you. Keep us safe and well In Jesus name. Amen.

In Closing:

◆ ◆ ◆

For the professional reading this book, May you find the hope that God has for you. May you know your limits are an open ground for God's exceeding and abundant hand. (Eph 3:20) May you know that God has not called you to do any of His work alone or in pain. May you know that it is okay to nourish your temple and take care of yourself. May you begin to find new and creative ways to gain peace as a professional and connect to the source of true strength, our Heavenly father the Lord God Almighty. May you remember the sabbath and keep it holy. Please know that God rested on the 7th day because taking time for self is essential to each of us. Follow the example of your King and take time for yourself before you lose hope. We are not meant to work harder than God, and we should not push ourselves beyond God's limits, or else we will lose hope because we are trusting in ourselves and not in Him.

God Bless the emergency dispatch workers. You listen to so many tragic crises at all hours of the night and still give your callers your best peace.

God Bless the adoption and foster care workers. You find direct care for children that have been wayward due to unsafe home environments.

God bless the school grief counselors. You give students a safe place to remember their classmates. You recognize the pain of seeing someone die too soon.

God bless the workers who take low wages and long hours to serve a population that is often forgotten.

7 Affirmations for the Christian Worker in a Secular Job

1. I am called to be the salt and light. My thoughts and actions will remain noble, pure, and admirable. (Matt 5:13-16; Phil 4:8)

2. God's strength is more than enough to cover my small faults. (Ps. 73:26)

3. God is with me and His Comfort is enough to get me through today and even encourage another. (1Cor 1:3-6)

4. God has plans for my future. I can trust Him, that it is safe to have hope. (Jer 29:11)

5. My steps are calculated for Good, God is prospering me. (Ps 119:133)

6. I can do every aspect of my job. I am strong, loved, and wise. (Phil 4:13; 2Tim 1:7)

7. I have no need to worry, When I'm in Christ I won't slip or fall. (Ps. 55:22)

RESOURCES FOR WORKERS:

Signs you may need professional help to deal with job stress

Next you will find a list of common work-related concerns and some resources on how to manage each matter.

Anger: When you find yourself irritated and prone to outbursts or arguments at home or work can be a sign that you need some time off for immediate self-care. Seek immediate emergency help if you are having thoughts of harm to self or others.

Anxiety: Worry and edginess about the future and the unknown can create tension and difficulty to control thoughts. A formal and severe case of anxiety may begin to interfere in your ability to work and function in your relationships.

Appetite changes: when you are no longer eating at

least 2 meals a day or you are eating food to comfort your emotions, consider talking with a counselor about how to better manage your stress. Unwanted weight loss and weight gain, as well as diet-related ailments such as diabetes and cholesterol, can be prevented if you learn how to manage stress-related appetite concerns.

Burn out: a common phenomenon that takes place when a worker feels ineffective in the job and start to wonder if the work is worth doing anymore. The day to day aspects of the job begins to outweigh the joy of doing the job well.

Chronic fatigue: When you find that you are tired at home and tired at work. Your energy to get things done is low in both places. This could be caused by stress about work or matters at home, but the end result is not getting enough rest and feeling low energy when you need it most.

Depression: Having sadness, hopelessness, and even feelings of guilt or worthlessness as a result of work stress is s serious concern. If you are thinking about harming yourself or someone else, seek out emergency care immediately.

EAP (Employee Assistance Program): A resource for employees to find help with emotional, social, and financial matters. Many companies offer EAP through a contracted provider , while others have EAP as a part of the insurance package. Contact your HR (Human Resource) department to find out more about the assistance services offered at your company.

Forgetfulness/impaired concentration and attention: This is when your ability to pay attention to detail at home or work diminishes. You may find that you are at a loss for words, or you just don't feel as sharp as you used to. In severe cases, you may find that you push important projects off hoping to come back at a later time. But you rarely find the time and forget to come back to the task. This is can weigh heavily on job performance and family obligations.

Insomnia: This is when you are not sleeping and you find that you are awake when you should be resting. Insomnia can be not being able to fall asleep or not being able to stay asleep. You should consult a doctor and or get professional help if you find that this occurs more than 2 nights in a row.

Isolation: This is when you prefer to avoid contact with others. This can be as simple as closing the office door at work, going to a room alone at home, or even avoiding phone calls from friends and family members that you once enjoyed talking to. If you find that you are changing your daily routine by early or late arrivals you may need support with managing the stress your work is causing.

Job Insecurity- This occurs when you find out that the position or department you are currently working in has changed in value to the company or industry. The company or industry may have a strategic plan to save or phase out the position or department you are in. This is a good time to find solitude with God and consider the best approach to take in finding out options to meet your career needs for a secure and stable income.

Low pay- Low pay is when you recognize that the work that you are doing is not receiving the compensation that your skills or training deserves. Some popular websites to determine the average pay for your field of work are glassdoor.com, indeed.com, and career-builder.com. These websites allow you to explore what others in your field with similar qualifications are making. They can also help you with creating a resume. However, you should remember to seek ye 1st the Kingdom of God and all this will be added onto you. If you are dealing with low pay, consider going to one of these websites to develop a resume and see what other jobs you are qualified for.

Physical symptoms: Work stress when highly severe, can cause physiological concerns such as High Blood

Pressure/ Decreased Immunity/ Frequent Colds or Flu/ Headaches/ Chest Pain/ Sore Muscles/ Stomach Problems/ Skin Eruptions/ Shakiness/ Dizziness/ or a need for self-medicating with substances like alcohol or recreational drugs. If you are experiencing any of these symptoms, you should consult a professional health care provider right away.

www.ingramcontent.com/pod-product-compliance
Lightning Source LLC
Chambersburg PA
CBHW031156250726
48655CB00002B/998